THIS BOOK IS DEDICATED TO ALL CHILDREN AND IN
PARTICULAR MY YOUNGER GRANDCHILDREN

EMMA, BELLA, HALEY, AND ZACHARY

DR. MONICA IS AN ANIMAL COMMUNICATOR
WHO LISTENS TO, AND COMMUNICATES
WITH PETS ALL OVER THE WORLD.

THIS BOOK IS BASED ON A TRUE STORY.

I ONCE HAD A DOG
HE WAS MY BEST FRIEND
WE WALKED AND WE RAN
AND WE PLAYED A GREAT GAME

HE WAS HAPPY TO SEE ME
'CAUSE WHILE I WAS AWAY
HE SAT PATIENTLY WAITING
AT HOME EVERYDAY

WE RAN ON THE GRASS
WE WENT FOR A WALK
WE SKIPPED AND WE DANCED
AND PLAYED FRISBEE A LOT

HE WAS SO SOFT AND GENTLE
A LITTLE BIT TALL
A LITTLE BIT SLENDER

HE LOVED TO PLAY DEAD
AND PRETEND TO BE SMALL
FOR THE WHOLE WORLD TO SEE
HE CURLED UP LIKE A BALL

WE WENT ON OUTINGS
WE WENT OUT SHOPPING
HIS NOSE WAS ALWAYS
PERKED-UP SMELLING SOMETHING

coffee shop

I DIDN'T KNOW HIM AS A PUPPY
BUT I ALWAYS KNEW
WHEN HE WAS HAPPY

HIS TAIL WOULD GO UP
HIS MOUTH WOULD BE OPEN
HE'D JUMP AND HE'D DANCE
AND HE'D RUN AROUND BARKING

SOMETIMES I SWEAR
I EVEN SAW HIM SMILING!

6

HE LOVED TO PUT
HIS HEAD OUTSIDE
THE LEFT SIDE WINDOW
OF DADDY'S CAR
AND IF YOU FORGOT
TO ROLL IT DOWN
HE MADE A FUSS
AND BARKED REALLY LOUD

HE BARKED AND MOVED
AND TURNED AROUND
AND ROCKED THE CAR
FROM SIDE TO SIDE

HIS NOSE WAS LIKE
A BLOODHOUND
HIS EYESIGHT LIKE
A GREYHOUND

HE COULD HAVE BEEN
AN IRISHHOUND
WITH EARS LIKE
A BASSET HOUND

THEY SAID HE WAS A MUTT
A LITTLE BIT OF THIS
AND A LITTLE BIT OF THAT
BUT IN MY EYES HE WAS
A FRIEND!
PLAYFUL AND LOVING
FROM BEGINNING TO END

THEN ONE DAY
HE COULDN'T MOVE
HE COULDN'T GO PEE
HE COULDN'T GO POOP

MY BEST FRIEND
WAS SICK ALL DAY
WE COULDN'T HELP HIM
WITH HIS PAIN

WE WENT TO THE DOCTOR
TO SEE WHAT WAS WRONG
WE WAITED, AND WAITED
IT TOOK SO LONG!

THE DOCTOR GAVE HIM MEDICINE
ONE PILL FOR MORNING
NOON AND NIGHT
THEN ONE MORE FOR THIS
AND ONE MORE FOR THAT
BUT NOTHING HELPED
TO CURE THIS MUTT

I TOLD MOMMY
I WOULD PRAY
TO MAKE HIM FEEL
LIKE NEW AGAIN

SO, I LOVED HIM
TILL THE END
AND TOLD HIM
I WILL NOT FORGET
HIS GENTLE KISSES
ON MY FACE
HIS LOVING PAWS
AND SWEET EMBRACE

HE WENT TO HEAVEN I AM TOLD
TO LEARN FROM ANGELS YOUNG AND OLD
TO VISIT ME WHEN I'M ASLEEP
AND CUDDLE ME SO TENDERLY

I SOMETIMES SEE HIM VISITING
FOR A BRIEF SECOND
WHEN LIGHTS ARE DIM
AND THEN I KNOW HE IS FINE AGAIN
BECAUSE HE IS NOW
MY SPIRIT FRIEND

MY GUARDIAN ANGEL
HE'S THE BEST
HE WATCHES ME
AND KEEPS ME SAFE
AS I LAY DOWN
MY HEAD TO REST
AND DREAM OF HIM
AS WE PLAY & JEST

I FEEL HIM WITH ME
WHEN I'M TUCKED IN
HIS BODY LAYS NEXT TO ME
HIS PAWS ON MY CHIN

MY GUARDIAN ANGEL IS INDEED
THE BEST FRIEND I'VE EVER SEEN

I DREAMT THAT HIS FACE
WAS SMILLING AGAIN
HIS BODY WAS HEALTHY
AND PERFECTLY WELL

HE RAN ON THE CLOUDS AND PLAYED CATCH WITH THE STARS
THAT FELL ON THE RAINBOW
ON TOP OF THE SKY

I WOKE UP EXCITED
AND KNEW IN MY HEART
MY MUTT WAS IN HEAVEN
AND HAPPY AT LAST!

WHEN A BEST FRIEND DIES

WRITTEN BY: DR. MONICA DIEDRICH WITH COLLEEN FOX

ILLUSTRATIONS BY: BMCREATIVESTUDIOS.COM

WWW.PETCOMMUNICATOR.COM

www.ingramcontent.com/pod-product-compliance
Lightning Source LLC
Chambersburg PA
CBHW061051090426
42740CB00002B/115